# Voice of a Songbird

# Voice of a Songbird

*Emily my dear —
I will always picture
you laughing and dancing
on the beach!!
thank you for
your Love,
your Songbird,
Nancy*

**Nancy Louise Mertz**

Copyright © 2009 by Nancy Louise Mertz.

ISBN:    Hardcover      978-1-4363-9306-5
         Softcover      978-1-4363-9305-8

All rights reserved. No part of this book may be reproduced or transmitted in any form or by any means, electronic or mechanical, including photocopying, recording, or by any information storage and retrieval system, without permission in writing from the copyright owner.

This book was printed in the United States of America.

**To order additional copies of this book, contact:**
Xlibris Corporation
1-888-795-4274
www.Xlibris.com
Orders@Xlibris.com

# Contents

| | |
|---|---|
| I Love | 11 |
| Confidence | 13 |
| Thanksgiving | 15 |
| 14 years old | 19 |
| May 2001 | 23 |
| Rainbow and Coincidence | 27 |
| Patio Visitor | 31 |
| Yes | 35 |
| Away | 37 |
| If Velvet Had A Sound | 39 |
| Tom is | 41 |
| I.C.U. | 43 |
| Molly Muffin | 47 |
| Early Fall | 51 |
| March. Still cold AKA: Silly Robins | 55 |
| A Broken Piece of Glass | 59 |
| Hoffbrau | 61 |
| Family Tree | 63 |
| Home From the University | 65 |
| My Christmas | 69 |
| To Jack . . . who is inquisitive | 73 |
| Guess Who | 77 |
| Sarasota | 79 |
| St. Paul's | 81 |
| Winter Insight | 85 |
| Wild Beauty | 87 |
| Scott | 91 |
| He is We | 93 |
| Giggling Gypsy | 95 |
| (Untitled) | 99 |
| A Cold Old Memory | 103 |
| After the Farm | 107 |
| Early Summer | 111 |
| Oklahoma Man | 113 |
| Can't Push Sad | 115 |
| Bundle Up | 117 |
| Music | 121 |
| | |
| About the Author | 123 |

To Benjamin Wilson Mertz
*un milagro*

*"Sing like you like to sing
God loves all simple things
for God is the simplest of all"*

*Leonard Bernstein*

# I Love

I Love
>singing the way I like to sing
>and being comfortable in boldness

I love
>being braless
>putting ketchup on tuna sandwiches
>and laughing loud

I love
>the ocean the sand the sun
>the first kiss . . . soft and slow
>black cashmere sweaters
>real butter on dark bread

I love
>faceted amethyst
>Gershwin songs
>his hands on me
>and ice cold lager in the summer

I love
>the last movement of Beethoven's 9th
>the smell of honeysuckle
>candles that burn well
>losing five pounds

I love
>a formata on a high B flat
>friends and margaritas on the patio
>a dog's warm head laying in my lap
>and making my mother laugh

I love
>being
>and
>hearing music in all things.

# Confidence

Full moon
and clouds tonight
and I think that's a nightingale
she still sings
even when it is very dark.
A good lesson.
To sing out even when it is very dark.
Now *that's* confidence.

## Thanksgiving

This is not a time of hibernation yet.

This is a time for learning new music,

getting to rehearsals, showing up prepared,

booking gigs, baking cookies, remembering

how much fun it all is, really listening,

breathing deep, feeling sexy, singing high

and strong, being gracious,

giving thanks.

If a singer opens her heart
the notes can soar and weep
in one breath

## 14 years old

When my son decides to talk,
he knows exactly how he feels about a thing
a book
a man
a meal
He is concise and clear and honest
with wording always beyond his years
talented
sincere
virtuous
He is fascinated with how different
people can be and seems to
accept them all. I have seen him completely
tolerant with the interruptive and aggressive,
the greedy and boring.
What amazes me is he never ever loses
his patience with the stupid,
and most smart people do, quickly.

But besides smart, he is forever kind-hearted.
An eternal blessing is this—
smart will get you far,
but smart and kind
will heal hurts
and move mountains.

Mending fences

    Mending is good,

        but it is still

            a fence

# May 2001

The azaleas are finishing and so are the lily of the valley,
just in time for the lilacs.

I took a two hour nap today, right in the middle of it. Yum.
Seems like everything comes in one day—errands, singing, choir,

commitments or rest. Feast or famine . . .
Grandma has endeared herself to me since her stay here.
Last night I helped her up the stairs to the toilet
where I dressed her for bed.

Then into bed with her little giggle and she reached out
to hold my cheek in her hand.
She says, "I love you dear heart thank you."
I kneeled by her bed and prayed out loud and then
we held each other and she giggled again.
Big blue clear eyes. Such loving and happy nonsense she talks about.

It will be a sad day when she is gone.
There is a peacefulness in being that old.
I think her days are no longer filled with the busy-ness of
taking care of little ones, or preparing meals or working.

Today we drank coffee together and she watched TV and napped
and watched the rain come down out the window.
She enjoys watching the activity around her—
me cooking a meal, Ben playing with the dog,
the girls in and out to work, putting flowers in a vase,
building a fire, having conversation, writing on the calendar,
answering the phone, cleaning up, brushing my hair . . . .
She watches it all with interest and complete contentment—
totally relaxed.

It's almost impossible to feel sad and sorry about her dementia—
her company is so peaceful and loving
and I prefer it to many clear-headed people I know.

Sometimes

someone can come into your home for one day

and everything is different

when they leave

## Rainbow and Coincidence

The other night the western sky was so yellow.
It was about seven pm, just after sunset.
The sky was windy and seemed to want to rain,
but never did.
I was with my dog,
looking at that surprising light in the sky,
and turned to walk home.
Boom, there was the rainbow.
A bright beauty. Humbling for the beholder.
I could see the complete arch,
a large colorful half circle.
I admired and stared and thought about you
sitting in the house, missing this.
So I started jogging,
and when I got to the corner of the street,
I could see your red jacket down the block,
in the middle of the road holding your camera up.
Rainbow and coincidence,

                a good walk.

I must remind myself
    that God is playing the music.
        All I have to do is
            be my note

# Patio Visitor

Rami came to visit yesterday

He was in the form of a striking
    white pigeon with brown wings.
    He was huge, and strutted with big
    slow steps across the patio.

I happened to be on the phone with Andrew,
    sitting on the back steps. I told him about this
    bold bird walking right in front of me, then
    stopping to cock his head and stare . . . and he says,
    "Hey, ya never know . . . maybe it's Rami saying hello."

I close my eyes and am reaching to
    touch his beautiful hair—black and curly.
    He laughs and his voice is rough from
    cigarette smoke. He is playing the guitar,
    then talking a mile a minute,
    going through his life like a meteor.

I open my eyes and stare back
    at the pigeon, knowing Andrew is right.
    I hang up the phone before the tears
    come and release my nagging and unsettled
    sadness
We hung out on the patio awhile,
    me and Rami.
        I'm happy for him.
            He always wanted to fly.

Many times I don't feel very strong

    but I end up doing

        very strong things.

            I see the same in my Mom

# Yes

Yes
to the rain
to singing high and sweet
to buttery green beans with almonds
Yes
to surviving unfairness
to being charming
to being stared at
Yes
to getting older
to feeling pretty
to smelling puppies
Yes
to the mess
and the clean-ups too
to the last day of school
Yes
to your silhouette at the grand
to the silence of the audience
to the thunderous sound of love
we are here together
a powerful duet

# Tom is

Tom is the tree,
the breeze by the brook,
the heron—staring, then in flight.
He is the sawdust flying up from the saw,
that valley on the way to Russell Brook
the shaft of light
that finds a place to shine.
Tom is heartache and frustration and insecurity.
He is deep and strong and listening.
He is dripping sweat
and numbing cold.
He is both high strung and exhausted.
His anger is quiet and so is his joy.
When his eyes see me,
they come straight to me.
They connect and lock into something
very deep inside of me.
Something powerful
and ancient.
It does not frighten me,
it is simply our way.
In my steady struggle for the freedom
to disconnect whenever I choose, somehow,
this is the man I come home to.
He is my fire,
the earth under my feet.

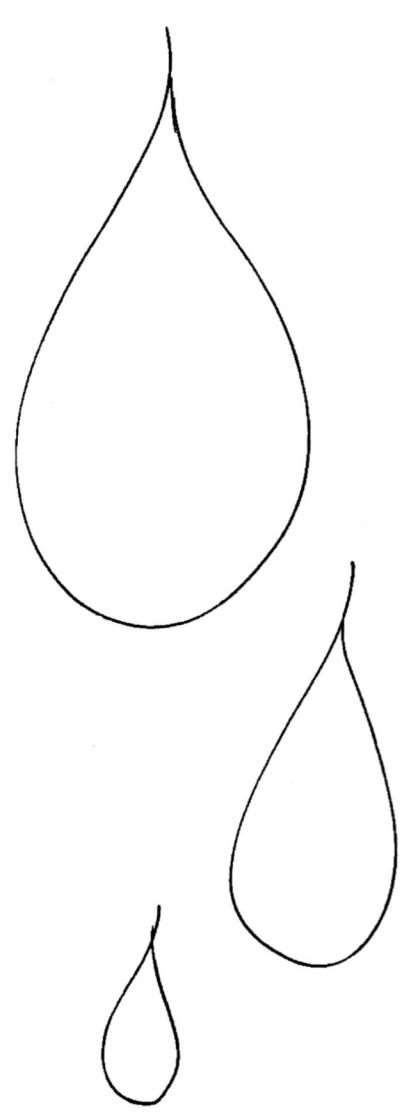

# I.C.U.

I ask him if he's ready to go
he answers with is eyes filled with
pain and a nod—yes
I tell him I understand, I love him,
I will sing for him, and I'm sorry he
has pain. Then I lay my head on his shoulder and cry.
I feel his hand, swollen from medication, squeeze mine.

A conversation so far beyond words
even the angels stopped to listen.

Once again real life strikes

a trampoline of emotion

## Molly Muffin

    My best friend weighs 39 pounds
and she loves to lick me right on the lips.
She is an excellent listener with big
dark eyes taking it all in. We have so
much in common—she loves to smile
and run and she is very drawn to other
animals, just like me. I am teaching her
how to sing. She doesn't care that I don't
like to cook. She is thrilled and thankful
when I give her one dry cookie . . .

    When I leave, she whines a very high pitched
breathy whine (I'm trying to incorporate this
natural talent into her voice lessons) and
when I come back she wags her tail so
furiously that her rear end swings back and
forth too. She is smart and patient. Her
love is deep and faithful.

    If she were a person, she'd be better than me.
She is the best friend a girl could ever have.
I wish we could live forever so we could
always be together.

One time I put a pair of sexy red panties on her, and took pictures. She is such a good sport, and didn't care that we all laughed at her. She loves to take naps and always wakes up in a good mood. This I find very impressive.

She has goals, too.
Her life long goal has been to catch a squirrel. Even if you say the word "squirrel" to her she is immediately in a state of hysterical excitement and needs to be let out to follow her dream.

It's wonderful to see someone doing what they truly love.

## Early Fall

We celebrate we listen we eat

We laugh

We clean we pet we bathe

We admire our work

We play

We call to the neighbors

We high five

We watch the fire

We live

VOICE OF A SONGBIRD

If pumpkins and bananas could have kids—

they'd be the colour of that moon tonight

## March. Still cold AKA: Silly Robins

So after the non-fight I plodded down to the field with the dog which was difficult since I had gained 75 pounds the night before . . . . the heart is a strong muscle to carry all that.

Slowly I tried a mental pep talk, and then I heard the birds. Loud chatting and flitting about the old Mama oak that stands alone. Many of them were robins. They think it's spring. Silly robins. I'm bundled up like an Alaskan. I kept walking and stopped and saw something that cut right thru my sarcasm and even made me smile.

Funny that something so dear and small and common could be so reassuring.

        I was saved,
                by the red-winged blackbirds.

Right now I am not free
      I am very busy
           doing what is expected.
There was a time when I was free

    and even my eyes
        had wings

# A Broken Piece of Glass

Whoa . . . . hold on to me . . . .
     on second thought
         let me fall.
  It's so soft and yearny
his hands are smooth
his eyes are crisp—and aqua
he is smart—but open
he does not judge—except himself
     he knows himself

Sometimes I can't sleep for the want of him.
Sometimes I can't eat and can only think of
     dressing sexy for him. Sometimes I am telling a
     story about him and my cheeks hurt from the
         smiling and my neck is red
             and I can't exhale very well.
Sometimes I think about telling him I am in love with him.
    I will wait.
Some men pick up love like a broken piece of glass.
    They can't trust it.
It is beautiful and shining clear but if they don't know
    how to hold it, it might slice right into their finger.
       But I would happily lay in his hand
    even if I were broken. I would smile up at him,
       assuring that
            my radiance
                would never cut him.

# Hoffbrau

High on friendship, we went out
to eat all the German food
        we could stomach

Bratwurst, and beer and red cabbage
and potato pancakes . . .
        I reminded myself that gluttony
            is one of the seven evils . . .

After searching my heart, I realize
    I have no remorse
           whatsoever.

## Family Tree

    I am the apple that fell
and then rolled away from
the tree to settle in the sunshine.

    They are organized and proper
and firmly planted; putting
strong houses up to protect
    from the wind.

I am dancing in the evening
    happy to let the wind lift
and carry me where it will.
    It has always had its own
      song.
But it is nearly impossible
    to teach an unbeliever
      to sing.

# Home From the University

All is right with the world
when Ben is home.
There is a reassuring steady peace
in the midst of my busy day whenever
he is here.
He is accompanied by more people,
more phone calls, more music in the house
more interplay
more discussion
more clarity
There is more me
when he is here.
Tomorrow my rainbow spirit will take a train
away from here.
My parents will see him off as I will be singing—once again
missing something because of my marriage to song.

I try to remember things are exactly as they should be here in the present.
After my performance I will sit in a pew and admire the stained glass
and then in my mind's eye I will see the departure . . .
I still like to picture a steam engine
puffing and chugging with a deafening whistle.
Mom will repeat over and over to him that they are proud of him,
and everything will be just fine.
Dad will repeat the logistics of traveling alone . . .
"don't keep your wallet in your back pocket", etc.,
then slip him forty bucks in case he needs a drink on the train.
Ben will be thankful and dear and smile and say,
"wow Grandpa, that's a lot of money for a drink !"
They will all hug a lot and Ben will say, "God bless" and be gone.
and I will get to the business of pretending
I am not lost without him.

In my spirit life

I am making friends

with Art Tatum's mother

## My Christmas

I give and sing and play and listen
and learn a new song and look pretty
and curl my hair and wear poinsettia jewelry
and stand tall and bow low and smile big
        and let everyone hear my laugh . . . .
            I buy and wrap and write and
send boxes and light candles and clean and
improvise . . . . I drive far and ring bells and
wear antlers on my head. I schedule and make
calls and cash checks. I stay up late looking at
the Christmas lights . . . they are admiring themselves
in my shiny black piano.

      I sing some more and feel thankful
and now
           there is only exhaustion.
              and one more thing . . . . a new love

VOICE OF A SONGBIRD

I am forever grateful

that I can put my arms

around (my) freedom and gently rock it.

## To Jack . . . who is inquisitive

You seem very concerned with what
I believe . . . and I know that you
are asking as a friend and not
one ready to weigh my heart
        against a feather

I believe in doing things if they feel good.
Laying nose to nose with my dog—
petting and thanking her for her
        deep devotion

I believe candlelight makes any face
        beautiful

I believe crying is OK . . . some of the
most likely places for me to cry are:
funerals, card stores, theatres,
Ben's performances, the ocean, and when
ever I am moved by true kindness.

I believe in angels
        I met one once
she had taken the form of a girl
        about nine or ten years old.
She was in an airport in Texas
        a great story for over coffee
    I always cry when telling it.

I believe music can heal hurts
    God has a sense of humor
    and that people really can die from a broken heart.

I believe in auras and visions and miracles.
I believe that every truth in the world
cannot be contained in one book.

I believe there is a deep connection between
women and the moon . . . we all come into our
fullness every 28 days . . . a sisterly coincidence.

I believe there are rich people who are
        spiritually homeless
    and Jewish people who are excellent Christians.

I believe in giving thanks and that
having faith in happiness can be a powerful thing.

I have never believed in begging for forgiveness.

I have always believed
        in Love

# Guess Who

He is so wise and wonderful
        and confident
                and thankful
                        and dear

He's a little Duke and a little Ghandi
        and Lord knows

                he was old when he got here

## Sarasota

It's February and things are blooming here.

Well worth the flight to feel the sun
      on my cheeks and shoulders
      me and Rez giggle and play
      together . . . after 40 years, we're
      gettin' good at it.

We were in a lovely courtyard today
      with lots of bright pink flowers and a
      HUGE likeness of David. I couldn't
      resist taking a picture of his black
      stone ass in the afternoon sunlight . . .

We drank wine, ate blue crab salad,
      shared all our secrets, and let the
      cell phones ring, unanswered.

We walked under those banyon trees
      with that thick hanging moss everywhere
      and those red-leaved lush plants
      in the shadows . . . an artist's dream . . .
            they said to me "Come . . .
                  rest . . . and feel beautiful"

                        so I did.

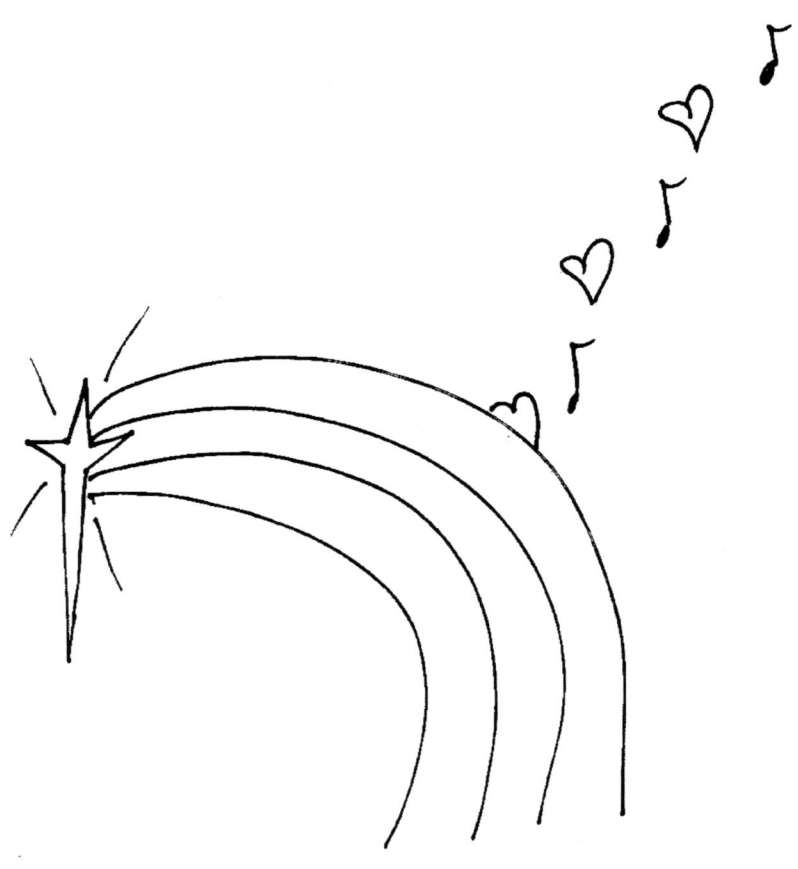

## St. Paul's

Cathedral singing. Beautiful moments.
So many colours and feelings in that church.
Always a lovely round tone that comes back at you.
Effortless . . . holding a high note

        singing is love on a vowel

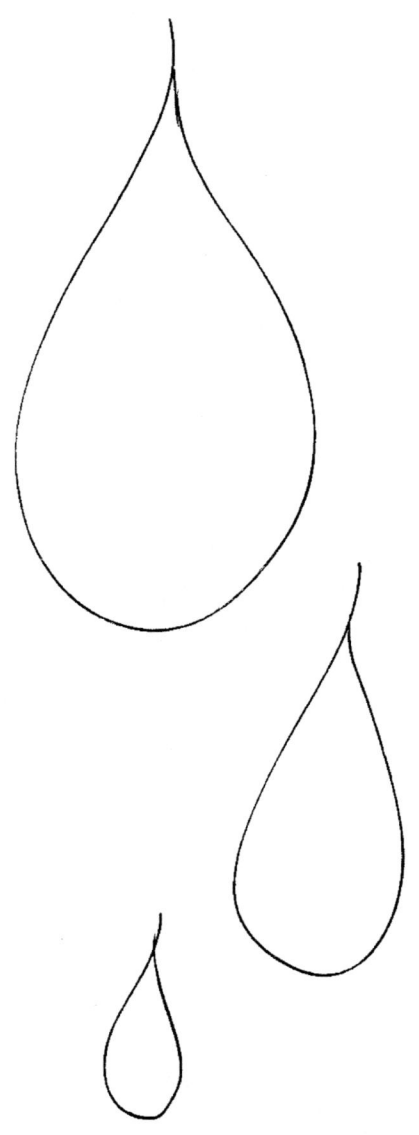

I try to listen to criticism

without getting hurt.

I cannot

I am only a child.

## Winter Insight

I used to think there was nothing
   more important than
      freedom
I would go to great lengths to achieve it,
including breaking hearts, quitting jobs,
     and traveling distances . . .
Now I am in a different place.
   Although potted and tied to a stick,
     I grow straight to the sun
and my fruit is the juiciest its ever been.
  There is a certain freedom
     after all
  in being delicious.

## Wild Beauty

Tonight I finally played the piano
after weeks of my hands being mute.
Whatever I wanted, and threw my head
back and sang like I was told was
         poor technique
but it feels so radiant and natural
I can't help but do it.
and then I looked at the picture of
you in my arms . . .
my my—what a photograph
taken with a long lens
when we didn't know it.
It was early summer and the G.W. bridge is behind us.
Your face says everything, wise wise consternation.
You are maybe four months old.
I am windswept
         and young
         and feeling like a wild beauty.
The problem now is
you are my music and you are gone
and something unstoppable happens
when I play the piano.
Our piano.
It swells within me, realizing
         how gone you are
and tonight I let it have its way
and I sang and belted and swayed
my songs of love and sorrow
and then wept. finally
         and walked and moaned
                  and I felt women from other places
                        with sons gone
                              moaning with me

I would have to agree

    with the ancient Egyptians

        that the act of spreading wings

           is in itself

                an act of prayer

# Scott

The way he looks at her

    she has waited many years

to see that 'I love you' truth

    melting in a man's eyes . . .

        chin in his palm . . .

He graciously relents to conversation

    but I know

    he would rather

    just look at her.

I am honored to be witness

        to a canyon so deep and silent

# He is We

I think that I am a good mother.
He is we.
He had tennis today, so sweaty,
hard to breathe . . .
Then to pick up a book.
Instead of rushing to the next errand,
we drank coffee and water sitting in the car,
reading, and looking at buds on trees.
He is we.
I play the piano and behind me in the street
he plays with the twins from school.
I hear him laugh.
I hear him breathing hard.
I hear him coming in for a drink.
I hear his heart,
    his thoughts,
       his pride.
I am driving him to a friend's house,
he is spending the night there,
so independent.
But I am with him.
I hear his voice.
I can feel his very heartbeat.
He is we,
he is true love.
I am the emotional fountain of youth
and he is wisdom and serenity,
always calming my worries.
He is we.

## Giggling Gypsy

Writing always begins with trepidation
    someone will read this
        someone will get their feelings hurt
        someone will be shocked.

    So I hold back
        to not hurt.

But then the gypsy inside rebels . . .
    perhaps she is selfish
        or just demanding

I am always aware of her,
    and am willing to let her have
        her time in the sun.

I try to be patient
    but also true

So I stick to the dress code
    but forego the underwear

        those are the days the
        gypsy and I giggle and hold hands

            and bask

What reason
would there be
to not live voluptuously?

## (Untitled)

Tonight it started coming up
after the movie
whatever it is that needs to come out.
The cause of infection and fatigue.
I run instead of crying.
I was strong and sweating
and salty.
If I start, it will be big.
If it comes, it will not end for a long time.
It would be loud
and very upsetting for a neighbor to hear.
I just cannot let it come
until I am out of earshot . . . .
away from my son,
away from my friends,
away from the people at work,
away from the driver behind me
away from the walkers in the park
I am never alone.
When I was young, the feelings would
burst out of me, totally unbridled—
sorrow, anger, laughter.
I am amazed at my control now
and so the emotions sit
and fester.

Crying things out

is very important, for sure

but singing

should always have

the final bow.

## A Cold Old Memory

You forgive and let it go

    and forgive and let it go

        but sometimes

           it visits

        and reminds you

    how cruel they were to you.

How dare they try to talk you out of

    being in God's hands . . . .

VOICE OF A SONGBIRD

I have lived enough to know

there are certain wars

that can be won

thousands of miles from the battlefield

## After the Farm

I love leaving—
the adventure, or at least the
possibility of one. The getting away.

It's coming back that's so damn hard.
This settled life. Dependable, predictable,
       unadventurous as hell.

He is the exact opposite. Nervous and
unsure about the leaving, never sleeping
well away from home.

      We get home and he springs to life—
      clinking and fussing happily around the
      kitchen
While I lay in bed cursing the
      lawn mower outside the window and the
      sirens across town . . . feeling the
      dead weight of the sunless sky
          on my chest . . .
wishing and wishing I were still away
      laying with the dogs
      licking and laughing
      and looking at
all those wide open acres
        of colour

One wonderful lesson
    life has given me is this:
        If one is a very very patient black sheep,
            one's wool can turn white.

## Early Summer

I gave myself to the sun today
    She held me a long time
        and reassured me
             all would be most well.

Then she kissed me
    and covered my face
        with lovely
            bronzed
                freckles

## Oklahoma Man

Yesterday we visited a friend.
She is getting a divorce after 31 years.
Her soon to be ex bought her a fine beauty
of a home where she hangs her
artwork and lives with her deep and
shaggy-headed son who is twelve. Her soon to
be ex came to the door to pick up the
wise one, so I went to meet him. There stood
this dignifiedtallattractivesilver-haired
gentleman holding a small dog. He smiled and
looked me right in the eye and that voice . . . .
that voice was so calming. I ask if he is from Kansas.
He is from Oklahoma. I am shocked that she is
divorcing this creature, but who am I to judge ?
Poor man—apparently he has one flaw which is
unforgivable.
I guess she had to run away. I don't blame her.
      No woman should die
           in a man's arms
                  from boredom.

## Can't Push Sad

Some sort of soft
sadness
is resting on me.
It is deep and sweet
and wants to be held.
It is rare to not want to sing or work
or bake or talk.
I suppose I will let it be
can't push sad
to change

## Bundle Up

Little by little we will once again make it through

the winter in the Northeast.

And someday after years of patience and dreaming

I will live in a warmer and friendlier place.

For now,

I will bundle up

and have faith

in the warming power of goodness.

What reason would be
good enough
to close the door
on an adventure?

# Music

To me, music is
    Lovely, warm
        continuing, unbridled
            a sacred balm
                a lifesaver

Breathing out perfection
    disciplined or rubato and free
        drilled or unrehearsed
            joyful or lamenting

It is time well spent
    like listening to rain on pavement
        or watching your baby sleep.

# About the Author

A native of California,
raised in New Jersey.

Studies piano,
voice,
and music therapy.

following her musical bliss
devoting her time to singing
and raising her son.

"Voice of a Songbird"
is her first published work.